MW00789716

New Believer's Series

1

WATCHMAN NEE

BAPTISM

Living Stream Ministry
Anaheim, California

First Edition, November 1997.

ISBN 1-57593-957-6

Published by

Living Stream Ministry
2431 W. La Palm Ave., Anaheim, CA 92801 U.S.A.
P. O. Box 2121, Anaheim, CA 92814 U.S.A.

Printed in the United States of America

05 06 07 / 10 9 8 7 6 5 4

BAPTISM

Scripture Reading: Mark 16:16; Acts 2:38; 22:16; 1 Pet. 3:20-21; Rom. 6:3-4; Col. 2:12

Baptism is a great subject in the Bible. We need to be clear about two aspects concerning baptism. First, before we are baptized, we need to be clear as to what baptism can do for us. Second, after we are baptized, we need to look backward and ask, "What is the significance of baptism?" In the first case, the baptism pool and the water are before us. As we are going to be baptized, we should ask ourselves, "What can baptism do for me?" After our baptism, we need to ask, "What is the meaning of my baptism?" One is a question posed in foresight, and the other is a question posed in hindsight. The former touches one's knowledge prior to baptism, and the latter, one's understanding after baptism.

I. WHAT BAPTISM DOES FOR A PERSON

"He who believes and is baptized shall be saved, but he who does not believe shall be condemned" (Mark 16:16). This verse shows what baptism does for a person.

A. Baptism Saving Man from the World

"He who believes and is baptized shall be saved." I suppose that all Protestants are a little afraid of this verse. Therefore, they dare not read it. Whenever they read this verse, they change it to, "He who believes and is saved shall be baptized." But the Lord's Word does not say this. In order to avoid the error of Catholicism, the Protestants deliberately go around God's Word. However, as they evade the error of Catholicism, they fall into another error. The Lord's Word is clear: "He who believes and is baptized shall be saved." Man has no authority to change it to, "He who believes and is saved shall be baptized."

1. Salvation Being a Deliverance from the World

Let us now pay attention to the meaning of the word *salvation* in the Bible. What is a person being saved from? According to the Bible, a man is saved from the world, not hell. The opposite of eternal life is perdition, but the Bible does not regard salvation as the opposite of perdition. The Bible shows us that salvation is one's deliverance from the world. As long as a person is in the world, he is already in perdition.

Let us consider man's condition before God. Today man does not have to do anything to perish. I will not perish because I have killed someone, and I will not be saved from perdition because I have not killed someone. The fact is that the whole world is perishing. From among the perishing ones, God has pulled us out and saved us. The whole world is perishing corporately, but God is saving men one by one, individually. God does not catch all the fish from the sea and then separate the good from the bad, assigning some to salvation while destining others to perdition. All the fish in the sea are perishing. Those which are caught by God are saved; the rest remain in the sea.

Hence, the matter of salvation and perdition has nothing to do with whether or not you have believed or how good your conduct is; it has to do with your location. If you are in the boat, you are saved. If you are still in the sea, you are perishing. You may not have done anything, but as long as you are in the world, that is enough for you to perish. It does not matter whether you are good or bad, a gentleman or a villain. It does not matter whether or not you live by your conscience. As long as you are in the world, you are finished. If you have not left that place, you are condemned by God.

2. Salvation Being a Matter of Position

Because Adam sinned and became a sinner, all men became sinners. Man need not sin to be qualified as a sinner.

All have become sinners through one man's sin. Today God has saved you from among many men. If you are on the world's side, no matter what kind of person you are, you are opposed to God, and you are God's enemy. Your position is wrong; it is a perishing position, one that leads to perdition. If you are a person in the world, you are perishing.

The word *salvation* has been used freely among us and with much confusion. There is a distinction between salvation and obtaining eternal life. Obtaining eternal life is a personal matter, but salvation is a matter not only of receiving the eternal life personally but also of coming out from a wrong corporate body. Brothers and sisters, are you clear about this distinction? Receiving eternal life is a personal matter. Salvation, however, is not just a personal matter; it has to do with the corporate body to which you formerly belonged.

Salvation means coming out of one corporate body into another. The receiving of eternal life speaks of what one has entered into; it does not speak of what one has come out of. Salvation includes both a coming out of and an entering in. Therefore, the scope of salvation is wider than that of receiving eternal life. It includes being delivered from the world, that is, coming out of the world.

3. Four Major Facts Concerning the World before God

There are four major facts concerning the world as shown in the Bible: (1) The world is condemned in the eyes of God, (2) the world lies in the evil one, (3) the world has crucified the Lord Jesus, and (4) the world is at enmity with God; it is God's enemy. These are the four major facts concerning the world before God. As long as a person is in the world, he is already condemned and will perish regardless of his conduct.

Please remember that the salvation of men is not a matter of personal conduct. They are wrong because their position is wrong. We know that it is not easy to be delivered from the world. How can I forsake the world if it is still attractive to me? However, when I realize that the world is in a wrong position with respect to God, I will have to forsake it no matter how lovely it may be to me. Hence, salvation is not just a matter of our personal conduct. The corporate body to which we belong is wrong. We need to be saved from our relationship with and our position in the world.

When the Jews tried to do away with the Lord Jesus, they cried, "His blood be upon us and upon our children!" (Matt. 27:25). Although we are not the ones who killed the Lord Jesus, our forefathers did. Even though we did not commit the act, the corporate body to which we belong did. The corporate body to which we belong is an enemy of God and is condemned to perish. Whether we are right or wrong individually is another matter. I hope you can see not only that we are sinners individually and need to be saved individually, but that we also belong to a corporate body which is wrong. The world to which we belong is God's enemy. The world we are in is condemned by God. We need to be delivered from that relationship and that position.

4. Salvation Being to Come Out of the World

What is salvation? Salvation is a deliverance from a certain corporate body. It is a deliverance from a certain position and certain relationships. In other words, it means to come out of the world. Most people pay much attention to their personal salvation, but the question before us is what are they saved from. The salvation highlighted in the Bible involves being saved from the world, not from hell. The world as a whole is condemned by God.

There is no doubt that he who believes has eternal life. We have been preaching this for many years. Once a person believes in the Lord Jesus, he has eternal life and is saved forever. All problems are solved. But please remember that if a person believes but is not baptized, he is still not saved. Indeed, you may have believed and you may have eternal life, but are you saved in the eyes of the world? If you are not baptized, you are not saved, because no one knows that you are different. You must rise up and be baptized, declaring that you have terminated your relationship with the world. Only then will you be saved.

5. Believing Being on the Positive Side, and Baptism Being on the Negative Side

What then is baptism? Baptism is a deliverance. Believing is on the positive side and baptism is on the negative side. Baptism delivers you out of that corporate body. Many people in the world may say that you are one of them. But the moment you are baptized, they will realize you are finished. The one whom they have known for years is now saved and baptized. Your friendship with them is terminated. You are in the tomb; you have reached the end of your road. You already know that you have eternal life. Now that you are baptized, you are *saved.* From now on, everyone knows that you are the Lord's and that you belong to Him.

"He who believes and is baptized shall be saved." This is true because once a person believes and is baptized, everyone will know where he stands. Without believing, there is no inward reality, and what one does will be nothing but an outward display. With believing, there is inward reality, and if one takes a further step to be baptized, he will be separated from the world, having terminated his relationship with it. Baptism is a separation. It separates us from others.

"He who believes and is baptized shall be saved." The Lord Jesus' word is quite clear. It goes on by saying, "He who does not believe shall be condemned." Unbelief alone is sufficient for condemnation. As long as a person belongs to that corporate body, his unbelief is sufficient for condemnation. But if one has believed, he still needs to be baptized. If he is not baptized, he still has not made an exit outwardly.

6. A Very Amazing Thing in the World

A very amazing thing in the world today is the attitude of Judaism, Hinduism, and Islam toward baptism.

Any Jew who embraces the Christian faith in secret will not be persecuted. Many Jews believe in the historical record concerning the Lord Jesus. Their greatest hurdle is not in believing in Him but in baptism. Once they are baptized, they are cast out. Some sisters were poisoned by their fiancé after they were baptized. Such things happen even in civilized communities like London and New York. It is all right for a person to believe in his heart, but once he is baptized, others will persecute him.

In India, no one will do anything to a believer if he is not baptized. But once he is baptized, they will cast him out. It is all right for one to believe in the Lord, but he cannot be baptized.

The reaction of the Muslims is more violent. Someone once said that it is difficult for a Muslim believer to remain alive. As soon as he believes, he will die. Dr. Swema is the first person who succeeded in working among the Muslims. He said, "My work will never grow, because once a person believes in the Lord, he has to be sent away immediately. Otherwise, he will die within two or three days after his baptism." This condition is prevalent even among Muslims today.

Baptism is an open declaration that one has come out. "He who believes and is baptized shall be saved." We should never consider the salvation here to mean a personal salvation of the spirit. In the Bible, salvation signifies a deliverance from the world, not deliverance from hell.

B. Baptism Being for the Forgiveness of Sins

On the day of Pentecost, the apostles told the Jews, "Repent and each one of you be baptized upon the name of Jesus Christ for the forgiveness of your sins" (Acts 2:38). The Protestants have difficulty accepting this verse. But this verse is the plain word of the apostles. "Be baptized upon the name of Jesus Christ for the forgiveness of your sins." It is strange that the emphasis of the apostle's word is not upon faith but upon baptism.

Was the focus of Peter's message in Acts 2 on persuading men to believe? No. Does this mean that Peter's preaching was inferior to ours? The Bible tells us that the most crucial thing concerning salvation is faith. How could Peter have left this out? Perhaps he could ignore other doctrines in his message, but how could he not speak about faith? Nevertheless, he did not speak about it. Instead, he spoke about baptism, and the Holy Spirit pricked the heart of those who listened. What about us? We say that faith alone is enough.

We think this is orthodox Christianity. Yet Peter said, "Be baptized upon the name of Jesus Christ."

Peter spoke only of baptism because those who listened to him were the ones who had killed the Lord Jesus. Fifty days prior to that, they were crying, "Take this man away." These were the same people who were shouting and crying in Jerusalem. Now they needed to be separated from the rest of the Jews. This is why it was not necessary to speak to them about believing. They only needed to be baptized. That would be sufficient for them to get out. As soon as they were baptized, their relationship with that corporate body would be terminated. As soon as they were baptized, they would leave that corporate body and their sins would be washed away. They would no longer be part of that corporate body; they would be out of it. This is why Peter said, "Be baptized upon the name of Jesus Christ for the forgiveness of your sins." The act of baptism brought them out. As soon as they came out, all problems were solved.

You need to realize that you were originally in the world and that you were an enemy of God. Since you have come out, you are saved. You need to confess before God and before men that you have come out and have nothing to do with that corporate body. You are through with it. "Be baptized upon the name of Jesus Christ for the forgiveness of your sins, and you will receive the gift of the Holy Spirit." This was the main teaching on the day of Pentecost. At this point your mind needs to be directed by God's Word, not by Protestant theology.

C. Baptism Being for the Washing Away of Sins

Let us consider the case of Paul. Ananias came to Paul and said to him, "Rise up and be baptized and wash away your sins, calling on His name" (Acts 22:16).

Paul was the foremost and greatest teacher, prophet, and apostle of Christianity. Was there a little error in his experience? Sometimes we preach the right doctrines but have the wrong experience. What would happen when we gave our testimony? What would happen if others did the same thing we do? The testimony of a teacher is very important because it may mislead others. Could it be that the experience of the foremost teacher of Christianity was wrong?

"And now, why do you delay? Rise up and be baptized and wash away your sins, calling on His name." Please take note of this verse. It says that baptism can wash away one's sins. The Catholics quote this verse and regard it as a personal matter before God. The error of Catholicism lies in saying, "If *you* are baptized, *your* sins will be washed away." Therefore, they claim that a death-bed baptism can wash away sins. They do not realize that the significance of this matter is not before God but before the world.

Formerly, Paul was a man in the world. After he had believed in the Lord Jesus and had seen Him, he needed to rise up and be baptized. The moment he was baptized, his sins were washed away. The moment he severed his relationship with the world, his sins were gone. If you are a Christian secretly and are not baptized, the world may still consider you as one of them. You may say that you are saved, but the world will not admit it. You may say that you have believed in the Lord Jesus, but they will say that they have not seen it. Once you get into the water, they will see it; they will know that you have believed in Jesus. Otherwise, why should a person be so foolish as to get into the water? The moment you are baptized, you are freed from the world. Water baptism is a severance of one's relationship with the world.

If a person believes in his heart but does not have any outward gesture, the world will still consider him to be part of it. For instance, in Kuling of Fukien there is a strong tradition of idol worship every fall; everyone is required to donate some money. If a person merely says that he has believed in the Lord, others will not believe him. But the moment he is baptized, they will know that he is no longer one of them. Therefore, baptism is the best way to free oneself from the world. If you want to be freed from the world, you must be baptized. You must tell the world, "My relationship with you is over." By doing this, you come out of the world.

Baptism is an open testimony, and we should not be afraid to let others witness it. Unbelievers can also be present during our baptism. Recently, when we baptized some people in Foochow, a brother said, “We do not like to conduct the baptism meeting in such a messy way. There were too many spectators.” If this is the case, John the Baptist would have to learn from this brother because John conducted baptisms that were not that orderly. Even the baptisms of the three thousand on the day of Pentecost were not that orderly. The issue is not whether a meeting is orderly. Of course, it is not good to be disorderly. But all the brothers and sisters should know what we are doing. When we baptize someone, we should let the whole world witness what we are doing.

D. Baptism Leading to Salvation through Water

The Scripture is consistent in its principles. First Peter 3:20 says, “In the days of Noah...a few, that is, eight souls, were brought safely through by water.” This verse shows us again that baptism leads to salvation. The Lord Jesus said, “He who believes and is baptized shall be saved.” On the day of Pentecost, Peter said, “Be baptized...for the forgiveness of your sins.” Paul’s action shows us that when a person is baptized, his sins are washed away. They are not just forgiven, but washed away. This is because our sins are washed away when we sever our relationship with the world. Here, the word in 1 Peter also shows us that we are saved through water. Therefore, baptism leads to salvation through water.

Those who cannot pass the test of water are not saved. A person who cannot pass through water drowns. During Noah’s time, everyone was baptized, but only eight souls came out. All the people were baptized and immersed in the water, but only eight souls emerged from it. In other words, the water became the water of death to some, but to others it was the water of salvation. Others go into the water and remain there, but we pass through the water and emerge from it. There is something positive in Peter’s word. When the flood came, everyone drowned. Only the eight souls in the ark, whom the water could not overcome, emerged from it. While the rest perished, these eight souls were saved. Today the whole world is under the wrath of God. For one to be baptized today means that he goes through God’s wrath. But he does not only go through it; he comes out of it. His emergence from it shows that he is one who has come out. This is baptism.

Baptism is being immersed on one side and emerging out of water on the other side. Baptism means passing through and emerging from the water. You must emphasize the aspect of "emergence." Everyone went into the water, but only the eight souls came out. Today we are saved through baptism. What does this mean? When I am baptized, I do not go into the water and remain there. Rather, I enter into the water and emerge from it. If you have never believed in the Lord Jesus, your baptism will not result in an emergence. Today my going into the water and coming out of it means that I am different from you. I can come out from the world through the water. I testify to others that I am different from the world.

E. Baptism Freeing Us from the World

The above four portions of the Scripture clearly show us what baptism is. Once we are baptized, we are freed from the world. We do not need years to be freed from the world. The first thing for a new believer to do is to be baptized. You must see the position of the world before God. You have renounced your former position in the world. This is salvation. You must put off the world completely. From now on, you are no longer a part of the world; you are on the other side.

Once we believe in the Lord, we should realize that we are no longer a part of the world. Our baptism is a sign that we are freed from the world. Through baptism we assume a different role. Henceforth, we abide in the ark and are persons on the other side. We can tell others that we do not do certain things because we have believed in Jesus. But, even more, we can tell others that we do not do them because we are baptized. We have crossed the bridge; we are on the other side.

Today we must recover the place of baptism before God. What is the meaning of baptism? Baptism means to come out of the world. It is a step which we take to free ourselves from the world. Our baptism is a declaration to others that we are out. This is like the words of a hymn which say, "Then the grave, with dear ones weeping, / Knowing that all life has fled" *(Hymns,* #628). Our dear ones know that we are finished and that we have come to the end of our road. We are through. Only this kind of baptism is effective. If this is not our realization, our baptism is too light and insubstantial. We must realize that we have been freed from the old circle and have come out of it. Eternal life is something that our spirit gains before God, but salvation is an act of our separation from the world.

II. THE SIGNIFICANCE OF BAPTISM

Everyone who is already baptized needs to look back and consider the meaning of baptism. Even if you were baptized ten or twenty years ago, you still need to review this matter. We should always remember the verse which says, "Or are you ignorant that all of us who have been baptized into Christ Jesus have been baptized into His death?" (Rom. 6:3). This verse is spoken in retrospect, not as a forethought.

The verses in Mark 16, Acts 2, Acts 22, and 1 Peter 3 are for those who have not yet been baptized, whereas the verses in Romans 6 and Colossians 2 are for those who have been baptized. They address those who have been baptized already. God is telling them, "Do you not know that when you were baptized, you died together with Christ and were buried and resurrected together with Him?"

Romans 6 emphasizes death and burial even though it also speaks of resurrection. Colossians 2 is more advanced; it emphasizes burial and resurrection, with resurrection as the focus. The emphasis of Romans 6 is death: "Or are you ignorant that all of us who have been baptized into Christ Jesus have been baptized into His death?" The main point here is death. We should die together with Christ. Romans 6 is on death and burial, whereas Colossians 2 is on burial and resurrection.

The water of baptism typifies the tomb. Today, when we put a person into the water, it is as if we are burying him in the ground. When we raise him up from the water, it is equivalent to raising him up from the tomb. Before one can be buried, he must first be dead. You cannot bury a living person. If a person rises up again after he is buried, this is surely resurrection. The first part of this truth is found in Romans, and the second part of this truth is found in Colossians.

A. A Great Gospel—I Am Dead

When the Lord Jesus was crucified, He carried us along with Him to the cross; we were crucified there as well. In the eyes of God, He has terminated us. What do you think of yourself? You may say, "I am a terrible person to deal with!" Those who do not know themselves do not realize how impossible they are. A person who knows God and who knows himself will say, "I am an impossible person."

When we were heavy-laden with sin, we heard of the death of the Lord Jesus. This is the gospel. Then we saw that we were beyond all hope and that we were dead. This is also the gospel. Thank God, this is the gospel! The Lord's death has included all of us. We are dead in Christ. This is a great gospel! Just as the Lord's death is a great gospel, our own death is also a great gospel. Just as the Lord's death is a joyful matter, our own death is also a joyful matter. What should be the first thought that comes to our mind when we hear that our Lord has died? We should be like Joseph of Arimathea; we should bury Him. Similarly, when we hear that we are dead, the first thing that we should do is to bury ourselves, because burial is the first thing that follows death. Death is not the end. We are already dead in Christ; therefore, the first thing we need to do is bury ourselves.

B. Having Died and Risen

Brothers, when we step into the water of baptism or when we look back after being believers for many years, we must remember that we are already dead. We allowed others to bury us because we believed that we were already dead. If our heart is still beating and we are still breathing, we cannot be buried. In order to be buried, we must be dead.

When the Lord was crucified, we were crucified too. We allowed others to put us into the water because we believed that we had died. The Lord Jesus has resurrected; He has put

His resurrection power within us. Now we are regenerated through this power. This resurrection power operates within us and causes us to be resurrected. This is why we rose from the water. We are no longer our former self; we are now resurrected persons. Today, we must always remind ourselves of this matter. When we went into the water, we believed that we died and needed to be buried. When we came up from the water, we believed that we had newness of life. Now we are on the side of resurrection. Death is on the other side, but resurrection is on this side.

C. I Am in Christ

Once I saw a headline in the newspaper which read, "One Person, Three Lives." The article was about a pregnant woman who had been murdered. After the woman died, it became known that she was pregnant with twins. Hence, the headline read, "One Person, Three Lives." Please note that concerning the Lord, it is, "One Person, Millions of Lives." This is why the Bible repeatedly emphasizes the words *in Christ.* In the murder spoken of above, the murderer apparently killed only the mother; he did not kill the two children. However, because the two children were in their mother's womb, they died when their mother died. Likewise, since we are in Christ, when Christ died, we died in Him.

God has put us into Christ Jesus. This is the revelation in 1 Corinthians 1:30: "Of Him you are in Christ Jesus." Since Christ has died, we are all dead. The basis for our co-death with Christ is our being in Christ. If we do not know what being in Christ means, we will not understand what dying with Him means either. How could the children die with their mother? They died because they were in their mother's womb. The analogy in the spiritual realm is even more real. God has joined us to Christ. When Christ died, we died also.

As soon as this gospel is preached to us, we should learn to look from God's viewpoint and acknowledge that we have died in the Lord. We have died because we believed this to be a fact. We have been buried in the water and have come out of it. We declare that we are on this side of the tomb. This is resurrection. Reckoning in Romans 6 involves both reckoning oneself dead in Christ Jesus and reckoning oneself alive in Him as well.

Brothers and sisters, I hope that you will take this way once you are saved. These are two separate thoughts. One thought comes before baptism, and the other comes after baptism. Before baptism we must see that we have already died and that we need to be buried. After baptism we must realize that we are in resurrection and that we can therefore serve God today.